RACE FEVER

Photographs by Glenn Seyforth

Text by Mark Baker

Above: Early photos from Daytona Beach (before a speedway had been built) and the Indianapolis 500 were destroyed by a fire that swept through my business on Jan. 6, 1988. Chippewa Falls firefighters had a tough time fighting the blaze, as temps were 22 below zero.

Left: Glenn Seyforth at Indy 500 in May, 2007.

Cover Photos
Top: Tony Stewart drives Car No. 20 into turn 1 at the inaugural running at the Disney World Speedway in Orlando, Florida in 1996.
Bottom: Ashley Judd, left, runs in the rain alongside husband Dario Franchitti after he won the 2007 Indy 500.
Portraits, top to bottom: A.J. Foyt, Richard Petty, Danica Patrick, Paul Newman, Kara Lazier, Rick Mears and Al Unser, Sr.

Foreward

It's been 60 years since Glenn Seyforth attended his first race at the Indianapolis Motor Speedway.

It's been 32 years since Glenn – a professional photographer – began covering the race for his local hometown paper, the Chippewa Herald-Telegram in Chippewa Falls, Wis.

In the intervening years, Glenn has snapped hundreds of photos of race car drivers, race car owners, track officials and general scenery in one of the most loved of American sports.

Race Fever is a compilation of some of the best of Glenn's photos from over the years. As an additional bonus, you'll enjoy reading the stories of how Glenn first became interested in car racing, how he won a $10 bet with speedway chief Charlie Thompson, and how one of the smallest daily newspapers in the U.S. came to have a seat in the new high tech media room in Speedway, Indiana.

If you talk to Glenn's wife, Arla, she'll tell you that while Glenn was off photographing races in Indianapolis, Daytona Beach, Milwaukee, Phoenix and Brooklyn, Michigan, she ran their business, a photo studio, and raised their three sons. Without her patience and perseverance, none of this would have come to pass. She truly has the patience of a saint.

In the spring of 2007, I approached Glenn about compiling the best of his work into a book. His wonderful photographs of the legends of racing, some still with us and others who have passed, are a national treasure. It is only fitting that they be shared with fans of racing.

A special thanks, too, goes out to the Chippewa Herald-Telegram's former owner, John Lavine, who first asked Glenn to photograph the races on behalf of his hometown newspaper. Without his encouragement, none of this would have come to pass.

So enjoy Glenn Seyforth's four decades of Race Fever photos.

Mark Baker
Publisher
Chippewa Valley Newspapers

Right: This photo holds a special place for me. In 1977, I was wandering around the garage area at Indianapolis and stuck my head in this door. Inside, race driver A.J. Foyt and his pit crew were working. "Are you with the media?" asked Foyt. "No," I replied, even though I had a camera around my neck. "I'm here to take pictures for my hometown newspaper." A.J. gave a quizzical look. "Isn't that the media? Every time I tell a reporter something, the next day I read it, and it's not right." I assured him I was only there to take pictures. Later that week, A.J. went on to victory, becoming a four-time winner of Indy 500.

ISBN 10: 1-59152-060-6
ISBN 13: 978-1-59152-060-3
Photographs ©2009 by Glenn Seyforth.
Text by Mark Baker.
Layout and design by Julie Nelson.

Produced by Sweetgrass Books, a division of
Farcountry Press, Helena, MT 59602

YT RACING
TEAM
4 TIME INDIANAPOLIS
500
WINNER
A.J. Foyt
KEEP
OUT!

Right: Race day 1979 Indianapolis 500.

Three encounters with Gene Autry

In 1940, when I was nine, my folks took me and my younger sister to see Gene Autry at the Minneapolis Aquatennial. Autry was a star of cowboy movies as well as a songwriter. Autry was the star attraction of a rodeo held during the summer celebration. As Autry rode his horse, Champ, I hung on the fence, trying unsuccessfully to touch the horse.

I had another encounter with Autry several years later, when I was about 12 years old.

After war broke out, Autry – like many Hollywood movie stars – joined the Army Air Corp. He toured the country during those bleak years to sell war bonds. In one of his stops, Autry appeared at Own Park in Eau Claire. Fronted by a big band, before making his pitch, Autry sang to a delighted audience.

As a newspaper carrier for my hometown paper, I decided then and there that I had to meet Autry in person.

I got a Saturday newspaper. It had a little write up about Autry's appearance. I took that Chippewa paper, got on the bus and went to Eau Claire. I got to the Hotel Eau Claire, went up to the desk and told the gal, 'Gene Autry asked me to deliver him a paper, and I can't remember what room he said he was in.'

She gave me the room number. I went up to the third floor and knocked. And he opened the door. There he stood in his bathrobe, all by himself!

And I said, 'Here's your paper.'

Autry looked at me for a second, and then replied, "Well, fine. Come in, come in. Have you had breakfast?"

I was surprised that the movie star would invite me into his room, much less to share his breakfast.

He was really, really great. I sat down – he had all those little stainless steel containers with food in them – and I had breakfast with him. I was so thrilled. I thought Gene Autry was the greatest cowboy that ever lived! And I still do!

That's not the end of the story, however.

Forty six years later, I encountered Autry again when Autry served as grand marshal of the Indy 500 parade. Autry was in the media room in May of 1989, surrounded by reporters from all around the globe, when I asked, "Do you remember when you were in Eau Claire, Wisconsin during the war?"

"I was never in Eau Claire," replied Autry flatly.

"Yes, yes, you were selling bonds," I said, trying to refresh Autry's memory. "You were in the Army Air Force."

"Well, I went to a lot of different towns, a lot of one night stands when I was selling bonds in the Army Air Force," said Autry. "So yes, maybe I was in Wisconsin. I just don't remember."

The rest of the guys in the media room were hanging on every word of the exchange. Autry was no longer a movie star and cowboy singer, but the multimillionaire owner of the California Angels Major League Baseball team.

I felt bad that Autry didn't remember being in Eau Claire, after I took the bus and got him a paper and everything.

Then Autry looked at me and said, "You've got an awful good memory. Would you like to manage a baseball team?"

The rest of the guys in the room just about died laughing.

Opposite page
Top: The famous Gasoline Alley as it appeared in 1978.

Bottom: Here I am posing with the 1978 Indy 500 pace car, a Chevy Corvette.

GASOLINE ALLEY
Revere
ELECTRONIC SCALES

OFFICIAL PACE CAR
GOODYEAR

PENNZOIL
PENNZOIL
PENNZOIL
CHAPARRAL
2
CHAPARRAL
GOODYEAR

Far Left: In 1979 at the Phoenix International Speedway, I stepped out on the track to take a great shot – and almost got my head torn off by track officials for getting in harm's way.

Top: Al Unser, Sr., pulls out of the pits in Phoenix in 1978. He is driving the same car that he used to win the Indy 500 a few months earlier.

Left: A close-up of Al Unser, Sr. in 1979.

Left: In 1981, the track at Indianapolis featured only bleachers. Suites were added later on.

Left: Johnny Rutherford signs autographs for fans at Indianapolis in the garage area in 1978.

Upper right: This is a photo of me when I was 12 years old, in 1943. Also pictured are my sister, JoAnn, and my dog, Pepper.

Falling in Love with racing

The year was 1946. For the previous four years, racing at the Indianapolis Motor Speedway had been suspended due to World War II.

Now racing was back.

As a 14-year-old, I was glued to the radio, listening to the race with my dad. Ralph Hepburn qualified for the pole at an astounding 133.944 miles per hour! This on a track designed for use at 90 mph. The thrill of racing flowed through the airwaves to Chippewa Falls, Wisconsin, where my family and I lived. I was hooked.

I listened as George Robson won in 1946. Mauri Rose won in 1947 and again in 1948.

In 1949, when I was 16, I sat down and wrote a letter to Wilbur Shaw, president of the Indianapolis Motor Speedway.

I wanted to be on a pit crew. So I wrote Shaw asking for a job. I got a nice letter back from him. He said the pit crews come with the cars, so I was going to have to contact someone who owned a car.

I didn't know what to do. I didn't know anyone who owned a race car.

But on the bright side, however, Shaw sent me a ticket to that year's race.

I decided I'd take the bus to Eau Claire. My folks were wild, telling me I was too young to make the 500-plus mile trip by myself to Indianapolis. But I was determined. I took to the bus to Eau Claire, 14 miles away, and walked out on to the shoulder of Hwy. 12 and stuck out my thumb. I hitched a ride from Eau Claire to Madison, and then a second ride from Madison to Chicago.

I got a ride around Chicago. This guy went out of his way to dump me on the other side of Chicago so I was out of any traffic danger."

That's when I hitched a ride with a young man driving a brand new green 1949 Olds 88. The 22-year-old's name was Bo Daily.

He should have been in the race, because he got me there so quickly. It was exciting and memorable.

Watching the old roadsters hurtling around the track at over 100 mph thrilled this small-town boy. Bill Holland won the 1949 race, driving a Blue Crown Special built in Crown Point, Indiana. I had taken a miniature Speed Graphic camera to snap photos of the race, and was puzzled to find that none of my pictures turned out. All were blurred, except one, as I found out later.

I didn't know what panning was in those days!

Stranger than fiction

Fifty years after I attended my first race at Indianapolis, I was back, taking pictures for my hometown newspaper, the Chippewa Herald-Telegram.

As I was walking in the pits, I spotted a man on the other side of the fence. I looked at him and said, 'How do I know you?'

He said, 'You don't know me!'

But I felt sure that I knew that face from somewhere. I asked him how he got interested in auto racing.

"I gave a kid a ride down here 50 years ago, and I've been hooked on racing ever since," the man said.

"Bo?"

The man replied, "How do you know my name?"

"You had a green Olds 88 convertible, and I'm the kid you gave a ride to 50 years ago!"

"Well," said Bo Daily, "I never would have known you, you've gotten so fat!"

Truth really is stranger than fiction. Who would've believed that 50 years later, I'd meet the man who picked me up and gave me a ride to my first race at Indianapolis?

It still brings a smile to my face.

Right: Bo Daily in 2000.

Top: Wanting to get a good shot, I climbed this boom tower to take photos during Carburation Day at Indy in 1979. I hit the down switch to get a better picture of Mario Andretti coming into Turn 1. An ABC TV employee gave me heck for fooling with his settings.

Right: A.J. Foyt pulling into the pits in 1978 at Indy.

Opposite Page: Al Unser, Sr. pulls out of Gasoline Alley in 1979, heading to the pit area.

GASOLINE ALLE
PENNZOIL
2

Top: In 1980, pit crews at the Michigan International Speedway didn't wear fire suits or helmets for protection.

Middle: Mario Andretti in 1978 at the Phoenix International Speedway.

Bottom: Herm Johnson drove the Spirit of Eau Claire at the Milwaukee Mile in 1980 for the Menard Racing Team, based in Eau Claire, Wisconsin.

Opposite page
Top: The so-called "snake pit" on Turn 1 of Indy in 1980 was known for drinking and carousing. In the 1990s, the snake pit disappeared when the race track built bleachers on this spot.

Bottom: The winner of the 1980 Indy 500 on the final lap – Johnny Rutherford.

PENNZOIL
4
GOODYEAR

Begging for more

From that point on, I would find a way to watch racing. When my parents went to Florida, I begged them to drop me off at Daytona Beach. Before the famous Daytona Beach Speedway was built, cars raced along the beach and down the sleepy town's Main Street.

Each fall, my family traveled to the Minnesota State Fair in St. Paul to watch racing. My dad enjoyed the sport, but he wasn't crazy about it the way I was.

My mother would pack a shoe box full of sandwiches. We couldn't eat out. That would cost money!

Most families in those post war days brought their own food rather than paying the exorbitant amount of 15 cents for a hot dog. My mother always packed a thermos of coffee for the adults and a big thermos of milk for my sister and me.

My dad parked by the track on the west end, right on the turn, and the dirt would fly through the air. When we'd get back to our car, there'd be two inches of dirt covering our car, and inside, too.

One of the more popular race car drivers in those days was Thomas (Tommy) Paul Hinnershitz, known as the Flying Dutchman, who hailed from Pennsylvania. Hinnershitz was coming into the Minnesota State Fair, driving a pickup truck pulling a trailer with is sprint car behind, when I spotted an opportunity. I jumped onto Hinnershitz's running board and lobbied for a job.

I pleaded with him.

"Take me with you, and teach me how to drive a race car."

"Son, I don't have enough money for me and my dad (who was crewing the race car for him)," said Hinnershitz. "I'd be glad to take you if I had the money, but there just isn't that kind of money in this business."

Years later, I would learn that sprint car drivers could earn tons of money, traveling the country, appearing at county fairs and state fairs.

Top left: A spectator on turn 1 of the Indy 500 keeps watch on the 1984 race from the top of a step ladder.

Top right: The start-finish line at the old Road America Speedway, Elkhart Lake, Wisconsin, in 1984.

Right: The Spirit of Eau Claire race car caught fire at the Michigan International Speedway in 1981, burning out three pit areas. Flames lapped at the fuel tank, background.

Top: Even when it rained, the race continued at Road America in 1986.

Left: Pit stop Road America 1985

Top: A bird's eye view of the garage area at Indianapolis in 1985.

Middle: It was a long, hot day for one spectator at the 1985 Indy 500, as he took a rest in a field along 16th Avenue in Indianapolis.

Bottom: After a hard day's race in 1985, a spectator finds a quiet place along a brick wall to catch a few winks at the Indy 500.

4TH ANNUAL DATSUN TWIN 200
ONTARIO MOTOR SPEEDWAY
APRIL 13, 1980

STARTING LINEUP - INDY CARS

		ROW 1	
4	Johnny Rutherford, Ft. Worth, Tex.	Pennzoil Chaparral/Cos.	196.803
11	Bobby Unser, Albuquerque, NM	Norton Spirit Penske PC9/Cos	193.473
		ROW 2	
5	Al Unser, Albuquerque, NM	Mark C. Bloom/Longhorn LR-1 Cos	193.187
1	Rick Mears, Bakersfield, Ca	Gould Charge Penske PC7/Cos	193.183
		ROW 3	
7	Tom Sneva, Spokane, Wash.	O'Connell Racing McLaren/Cos	192.967
10	Pancho Carter, Brownsburg, Ind.	Alex Foods Penske PC7/Cos	190.702
		ROW 4	
40	Tom Bagley, Centre Hall, Pa.	Patrick Racing Penske PC6/Cos	189.561
20	Gordon Johncock, Tempe, Az.	Patrick Racing Wildcat/Cos	187.570
		ROW 5	
55	Spike Gehlhausen, Indianapolis	Fletcher Racing Penske PC7/Cos	187.145
14	A.J. Foyt, Houston, Tex.	Gilmore-Foyt Parnelli/Cos	186.889
		ROW 6	
69	Joe Saldana, Brownsburg, Ind.	Offman Penske PC7/Cos	186.339
48	Mike Mosley, Fallbrook, Ca.	Theodore Eagle/Cos	185.594
		ROW 7	
72	Roger Mears, Bakersfield, Ca.	Hodgdon National Eng/McLaren/Cos	181.52
60	Gordon Smiley, Dallas, Tex.	Patrick Penske PC6/Cos	181.236
		ROW 8	
41	Bill Alsup, Woodstock, Vt.	Alsup Racing Penske PC7/Cos	180.422
38	Rick Muther, Laguna Beach, Ca.	Pacific Racing Team/Penske PC6/Cos	178.[illegible]
		ROW 9	
~~23~~	~~Dick Ferguson, Glendale, Ca.~~	~~Aero Electronics & Gallcs~~	
		Chevrolet Penske PC6/Cos	176.512
15	Bill Tempero, Fr. Collins, Colo.	Spirit of Colorado Eagle/Chevy	173.910
		ROW 10	
47	Phil Caliva, Hermosa Beach, Ca.	Alsup Racing McLaren/Offy	173.779
24	Sheldon Kinser, Bloomington, Ind	Leader Cars & Scientific Drilling Watson/Offy	170.091
		ROW 11	
34	Pete Halsmer, Huntington Beach, Ca.	Wysard/Autocraft Wildcat Offy	169.122
28	Herm Johnson, Eau Claire, Wis.	Spirit of Eau Clair Lightng/Offy	166.56[illegible]

NON QUALIFIERS: # 75 Ron Shuman 165.786
#50 Jan Sneva 163.328
#22 Ross Davis 163.085
#42 John Wood 159.618

Right: Driver Tim Richmond, shown here in 1987 at Indy, later left open wheel racing to go into stock car racing. Richmond died in August, 1989.

Opposite Page:
Top: Race car drivers Mario Andretti, left, A.J. Foyt, center, and Michael Andretti, right, pose with their cars and pit crews before the 1987 Michigan 500.

Bottom: Nine past winners of the Indy 500 pose before the 1987 race in front of the Borg-Warner Trophy.

HANNA
KRACO
STP
5
14
18

BORG-WARNER
Bud

Right: Danny Sullivan pulls into the pits at the Road America racetrack in Elkhart Lake, Wisconsin in 1988.

Bottom: Jim Gilmore, who sponsored A.J. Foyt for years via Gilmore Racing, is shown at the 1989 Indy 500.

A sparrow, a $10 bet & Charlie Thompson

When I returned from the 1949 Indy 500 race, I wanted to do something special for Wilbur Shaw. Shaw, after all, sent a 16-year-old boy a ticket to that year's race – an offer that I took advantage of.

Back home in Chippewa Falls, I developed the film I had taken at the racetrack with my miniature Speed Graphic camera in the basement darkroom my grandfather had made for me.

I was shocked at what I found. With race cars hurtling by at 100-plus miles per hour, my photos were blurred. I did not yet know how to pan my camera, tracking the cars while pressing the shutter to keep the car in focus while the background blurs.

One photo did, however, stand out. I snapped a perfectly focused photo of a sparrow, resting on the fence. The blur of Bill Holland's Blue Crown Special racecar sped by in the background, accentuating the speed of the race.

I made an 11x14 print of the photo, carefully applying my "Photo by Glenn Seyforth" stamp to its back. Bud Padrutt, owner of the photo studio where I worked part time, helped me matt and frame the photo. Then we covered the back with brown paper to prevent dust and dirt from entering. I mailed the finished product to Wilbur Shaw, and forgot about it for nearly three decades.

In 1977, Chippewa Herald-Telegram owner John Lavine asked me to cover the Indy 500 for his small town daily. I represented one of the smallest newspapers in the U.S. to be credentialed by the race track.

That fall, I suffered a heart attack. When I returned to Indianapolis for the 1978 race, I inquired about getting a parking spot close to the garages so I didn't have to walk so far.

Roger Dupray, in charge of press credentials, agreed to help me get a closer parking spot. He advised me to go to Charlie Thompson's office to work it out.

Thompson was director of the speedway, in charge of everything from vendors to security. Thompson's office was located in the back of the museum.

As I came into the office area, I spotted a picture hanging on the wall. It was of the sparrow with Bill Holland speeding by – my picture from 1949.

"I took that picture," I told Thompson.

That, Thompson said, wasn't possible.

"That was taken back in the '40s."

I agreed.

"I know. I sent it to Wilbur Shaw to thank him for sending me a ticket to attend the 1949 Indy 500."

Charlie would have none of it.

"I'll bet you didn't," said Thompson.

I was now in too deep to back out.

"How much (do you want to bet)?"

(Note from Arla Seyforth: "When Glenn bets, you know it's a sure thing!")

Ten bucks, said Thompson, who wondered how in the world I would be able to prove that I took the photo.

"Let me look at the back of the picture."

Thompson took it down from the wall. I turned it over, and was relieved to see that there wasn't any indication that the paper backing had been cut.

"We have to take the back off, and if my rubber stamp is there, you owe me ten bucks!"

I worried that after nearly 30 years, the ink from my stamp may have faded and disappeared. I carefully removed the brown

paper backing, and – sure enough – there clear as can be was the stamp, "Photo by Glenn Seyforth."

From that day on, Charlie Thompson complained that it wasn't a fair bet. I still laugh at the ugly scowl Charlie would shoot my way whenever I tried to take his picture.

He was absolutely a great man. I thought the world of him.

Left: Charlie Thompson lost a $10 bet to Glenn over a photo of a sparrow.

Right: Comedian Jay Leno drove the pace car in 1999 at Indy.

Top: Jay Leno poses for a photo in the 1999 pace car.

Bottom: Mary George, whose family owns the Indy 500 track, is shown in 1987.

Top left: Actor, race car driver and race car owner Paul Newman eats popcorn at the Indy track in 1985.

Right: Newman is interviewed by ESPN at Road America in Elkhart Lake, Wisconsin in 1985.

Rubbing elbows with a few celebrities
A tribute to Paul Newman

Over the years, I got to meet quite a few celebrities while covering races.

One of my favorites was the actor and race car driver Paul Newman.

In 1969, Newman came to Indianapolis to film the movie, Winning, about a race car driver.

It was one of the finest pictures I ever saw. Paul enjoyed making the movie because he loved auto racing.

Newman converted from an actor/amateur to a real life professional driver, competing in his first race in 1972. He later drove for the Bob Sharp Racing team, and then formed his own racing team. Newman and a partner, Carl Haas, formed Newman/Haas racing, running Champ cars.

Paul didn't like many of the photographers who followed him around, as they made a spectacle of trying to get his picture. I never did that.

One time, while covering the Road America race in Elkhart Lake, Wis., Paul took me aside and gave me the ultimate compliment.

"I'm not too big on photographers who are always in your face," Paul said. "You've never done that, and I appreciate that."

Paul was a good race driver and a humanitarian. He would never take credit for all the good he did. The profits from his popcorn and salad dressing companies went to a variety of charitable causes.

He took care of youth. He built centers for them, and never took credit for it. He wasn't egotistical. He didn't want people to know he did this or he did that. He didn't want praise. He was just a wonderful, down-to-earth person.

Top left: Actor James Garner is shown in 1990 with Jim Rathmann, winner of the 1960 Indy 500. Rathmann is the oldest living winner of the Indy 500.

Top right: Donald Trump at Disney World in 1996.

Left: In 2006, bicycle racing champion Lance Armstrong drove the Indy pace car.

When race car owners split between the Indy Racing League and Champ cars, Newman and Haas went with Champ cars. Just before Newman died in 2008, Newman/Haas returned to the speedway with the merger of the two leagues.

I wish he would have lived long enough to see the success of the two coming back together.

Other celebrities

Over the years, I was able to photograph a number of other celebrities. TV actor Jim Nabors came back yearly to sing "Back Home in Indiana" prior to each race. A great guy!

Sometimes, I didn't even recognize some of the stars.

In 1979, I was sitting on the wall, visiting with Jim Hall, owner of a Chaparral car.

There was a lot of activity around this one fellow. So I asked Jim who it was.

"That's John Travolta," said Hall. "He had just made Urban Cowboy."

In 2008, I sat next to the fellow who had driven the pace car. Again, I didn't know who he was. Listening to the crowd's reaction, I turned to him and said, "Either all that applause is for you or for me!"

Patrick Dempsey, star of Grey's Anatomy, got quite a kick out of that.

Way back in the early days, I was covering a race at the Phoenix International Raceway. After a long day of shooting, I went for dinner to the Pink Horse Ranch in nearby Scottsdale.

Actor Phil Harris was already parked at the end of the bar, enjoying a drink.

Harris asked if I knew the baseball celebrity sitting on the barstool next to me. I turned and looked. Apologizing, I said that he really didn't follow baseball that closely.

"I'm not a big baseball fan."

"Don't say anything to the guy next to you, because he's liable to knock you off the stool and kick dirt on you," Harris hollered.

"Do you know who I am?" the man asked me.

"No," said I.

"I'm Billy Martin. Does that ring a bell?"

"No, sorry."

"I'm the manager of the New York Yankees, and he's (Harris) making a little joke because I had a run in with an umpire."

New York Yankees manager Billy Martin was famous for his hot temper, championship teams, and full frontal assaults on umpires.

Billy was a very nice person, but Phil Harris had to have his fun.

Upper left: John Cougar Mellencamp, 2001.

Bottom left: Marla Maples, 1996.

Opposite page
Top: Dave Letterman, center, visits with driver Bobby Rahal prior to the 1988 Indy 500.
Bottom: Ashley Judd smiles during a practice round in 2002.

Bud
KING OF BEERS
symbolics
NEWS
PHOTO

Right: Jim Nabors waves to the crowd at the 1997 Indy 500 after singing, "Back Home in Indiana."

Top left: John O'Reilly, left, of Johns Manville, poses with John Menard, owner of the Menard's Racing Team. Johns Manville is a sponsor of Team Menard.

Top right: Singer Wynona Judd watches the action at Indianapolis in 2003.

Left: Actor Jim Nabors, left, enjoys a laugh with comedian Ruth Buzzi and Florence Henderson at a Saturday morning driver's meeting at Indy.

Top: Changing tires in the fast lane at the 2000 Indy 500.

Right: Driver Juan Montoya looks on as his race car is serviced in the pits at Indy in 2000.

Opposite Page: Kara and Buddy Lazier, winner of the 1996 Indy 500, pose at the time trials at the Indy 500 in 2006.

28 27
29 93
30 18
31 16
32 26

Top: Robby Gordon is shown during the 2000 Indy 500 race.

Middle: The Harrah race car comes in for a pit stop during the 2000 Indy 500 race.

Bottom: Driver Greg Ray and Team Menard prepare for the 2000 Indy 500.

Top left: Eddie Cheever, left, winner of the 1998 Indy 500, waves to the crowd during his victory lap as race track president Tony George looks on.

Right: Kara Lazier, wife of race car driver Buddy Lazier, watches the action during the 2004 race.

Developing a friendship with Rick Mears

One of the benefits of spending time at the Indy racetrack is getting to know the owners, drivers and support crews as people.

In 1977, race car owner Roger Penske brought Rick Mears, a young off-road racer, into his organization. I met Rick that year at the Phoenix International Raceway.

He was there, but not as a driver. I took some pictures of him and Roger Penske.

Instantly, Rick and I took a liking to each other.

Out of all the race drivers, I got to know Rick best, along with his father, his mother and his brother, Roger. I used to sit on the wall with him and we'd talk about different things every year.

In 1978, I watched as Mears qualified for the outside of the first row at Indy. The next year, I saw Mears come back and win the Indy 500 for the first time.

Rick came from tough stock. One year, Rick's father and mother were sitting down to lunch in their recreational vehicle at Indianapolis when the door flew open. A bandit accosted the pair, demanding money.

It had been me, I would have fainted.

Rick's mom, however, took matters into her own hands. She jumped up and grabbed a hold of the would-be-robber, who panicked and fled from the scene.

They could have been shot! It really was a terrible thing. They were very, very lucky people.

One of my favorite Indy races occurred in 1982.

PENNZOIL
2
Hertz
MONROE
GOODYEAR
GOODYEAR
MONROE
PENNZOIL

Page 47: Rick Mears's crew fuels his car during an Indy 500 race.

Top left: Rick Mears speaks with a member of his crew at the Phoenix International Speedway in 1979.

Top right: Chris and Rick Mears at the Indy 500 in 1990.

Left: Rick Mears, winner of the 1979 Indy 500, poses with Glenn Seyforth after the race.

Mears and Gordy Johncock battled each other throughout the race. The lead changed hands often.

I knew that Rick was going to be able to overtake Johncock. Rick never drove 'over the line.' He always raced so he wouldn't crash.

Gordy Johncock was just strong enough that day, in that Pat Patrick car, that Rick absolutely couldn't get by him. It was so exciting, and everyone was standing. Those last few laps were unbelievable. I felt like everyone else, that Rick was going to get by him.

In the end, it came down to the final two laps. When their cars hurdled across the finish line, Johncock ended up winning by less than a tenth of a second.

Johncock won the race, but Rick was right on his tail. When Rick talked about the race afterwards, he was a gracious loser.

He gave Gordy all the credit. What a super driver.

Eventually, Mears would end up winning four Indy 500 races, tying him with legendary drivers A.J. Foyt and Al Unser, Sr.

He should have won five races. Rick will probably go down as one of the greatest drivers of all time.

Miller
AMERICAN
PPG
UNSER
PENNZOIL
5

Opposite Page: Rick Mears visits with Al Unser, Sr., at Road America in 1985.

Top: Bill Mears (center) father of Roger and Rick gives a bit of advice to his grandson, Casey, in 2003.

Middle: Rick Mears, left, with his nephew, Casey, at the Brickyard in 2003.

Bottom: Rick Mears at the Indy 500 in 2005.

Top: Jan Shaffer, left, IMS public relations, visits with Bill York, who supervised the media room, at the 2003 Brickyard 400.

Left: Tom Carnegie, the Voice of the Indy 500, smiles as he reads a copy of the *Chippewa Herald* featuring Glenn's photos from the 2003 event.

Top left: Janet Revoir, left, and her sister, Annie White, right, are from my hometown of Chippewa Falls, Wisconsin. They now work crowd control at the Indy speedway.

Top right: Pit stop action in during Formula One racing in 2003 in Indianapolis.

Left: Smell the rubber burn during the 2004 Indy 500 race as a Johns Manville car takes off from a pit stop.

Right: Jim Hanson, a friend of mine from Chippewa Falls, poses on the Indy 500 track in 1984 holding his infamous pair of binoculars.

Pulling Jim Hanson's leg from 100 years away

I met Jim Hanson at The Flame restaurant in 1977. Hanson was, at the time, co-owner of Car City Honda in Chippewa Falls.

We were talking about auto racing. It quickly became obvious that Hanson shared my passion for auto racing.

Seeing that he loved racing so much, I suggested that Hanson join me when I went to the next Indy 500 race.

Hanson signed on as my assistant that year, the same year A.J. Foyt won his fourth race.

We were in the garage area the Friday before the running of the pole. There was a beautiful Starcraft van parked there. I noticed that on the lower corner of the back panel was a chrome plate that said 'Armstrong Racing.'

Saturday night, we went to the Indiana State Fairgrounds for the running of the Hoosier 100, a sprint car race. Hanson took out a pair of field glasses and began scanning the area. In the infield, about 100 yards away, Hanson spied a nice looking vehicle.

"That's one beautiful van on the infield," he remarked.

I squinted my eyes and calmly said, "There's a plate on the back that says – let me see if I can make it out – oh, yes, it says 'Armstrong Racing.' "

Hanson looked at me as if I was out of my mind.

"You can't see that!" he exclaimed "You must have seen that van somewhere else!"

No, I replied, I didn't, and I was pretty sure about what it said. But just to be sure, I asked Hanson to lend me his set of field glasses.

Peering through the binoculars for a few seconds, I said, "Yes, that's what it says – Armstrong Racing!"

"You saw it somewhere else!" Hanson cried.

"No," I responded, "I've just got real good eyes."

It took a few days – and countless accusations later – before I finally 'fessed up to what had really happened.

Opposite page:
Top: Cool colors during the 2002 Indy 500.

Bottom: Pit stop for the Menard's Racing Team during the 2002 race in Colorado.

RACE
SPEC
Indianapolis Motor Speedway

MOEN
MENARDS
2
BOSCH
KLOTZ
EARL'S

Above: Green-helmeted pit crew members change tires during Vitor Mera's pit stop during the 2003 Indy 500.

Opposite page: Helio Castroneves and his crew climb the fence after he won his first Indy 500 in 2001.

Marlboro

Left: Tom Sneva drove for John Menard in 1992. Sneva later went on to own a golf course in Arizona.

1978– Tom Sneva gives me the ride of my life

Most members of the media and public never get a chance to experience the true thrill of auto racing.

We watch from the stands, or on our television sets, as the cars thunder down the straight-aways and around the track.

In 1978, I got a chance to experience the race track in a special way.

I got to know race car driver Tom Sneva when I did photography work for him. Tom owned a golf course in Arizona, and as a professional photographer, I took pictures of the course for Sneva and Ping.

So it was not unusual when we exchanged pleasantries at the track the Friday before qualifying runs in 1978.

"Do you want to take a ride with me in the pace car?" Sneva asked.

I looked at the pace car - a gorgeous black and silver 1978 Corvette.

"Sure!" I said.

Seeing the tiny 8mm movie camera I was carrying, Sneva suggested I bring it along so that I could film what it was like to barrel down the speedway. Back home in Wisconsin, I would show photos and film from Indy 500 to civic groups and schools. It reinforced my message that one couldn't do drugs and be a professional race car driver.

So when Sneva made the offer, I took him up on it.

"It will give you an idea of what the track looks like when we go around a few laps," Sneva said.

I climbed in to the Corvette, looking forward to the experience. Like most people, I had never driven – or ridden – in a car traveling over 100 miles per hour in my life.

It didn't take Sneva long to exceed the 100 mile per hour barrier. As the car barreled down the track, Sneva looked over at me – and I was frozen in place, the camera in my lap, my arms unable to move.

"When are you going to start taking pictures?" Sneva inquired.

I shot him a look that could kill, if only I could move any part of my body.

I was just petrified. I had the camera in my lap, and I couldn't pick it up!

The worst part was on the turns, when the pace car floated up within inches of the wall as it roared ahead.

That year, Sneva was made for speed. The very next day, Sneva became the first driver ever to break the 200 mile per hour barrier for four laps, earning the pole position for Sunday's race.

When Sneva came out of turn 4 during qualifying round, I know he touched the wall. But he never took his foot off the gas. He came through and won the pole position at better than 200 mph for the four laps.

For the next several years, every time Sneva ran into me, he would gently tease me.

"Let's take a little ride in the pace car," Sneva would say.

Top: Tom Sneva, left, was the first driver to average more than 200 mph at the Indy 500 in 1978.

Middle: Tom Sneva is pictured at the Phoenix International Raceway in 1978.

Bottom: Tom Sneva and his wife, Diann, are pictured taking the victory lap after the 1983 Indy 500.

Top left: Felipe Giaffone drove for Dreyer & Reinbold Racing in the 2004 Indy 500.

Top right: Michael Schumacher's Ferrari garage is drenched in red for the 2003 Formula 1 race at Indy.

Left: Ward Burton prepares for qualifying at the 2004 Brickyard.

Top: Dale Earnhardt, Jr., is in the garage at the Michigan International Speedway in 1988.

Bottom: Kara Lazier, wife of driver Buddy Lazier, at the 2005 Indy 500.

Right: Bobby Labonte drove a bright green Monte Carlo for Interstate Battery in the 2003 Brickyard.

42
MBNA
MBNA
INTERSTATE BATTERIES
JOHN 3:16
18
INTERSTATE BATTERIES
NASCAR

1988– Playing a practical joke on David Letterman

I occasionally played practical jokes on celebrities who came to watch the Indy 500.

David Letterman, a native of Indianapolis, loves car racing. The late night star of the CBS show named after him regularly came back home to watch the big race.

On his TV show prior to the 1988 race, however, Letterman began poking fun of driver Bobby Rahal. He teased Rahal that he'd never make it in racing. Once, his show even constructed a set with a single light bulb, with Letterman interviewing a faux Rahal and poking fun at his efforts.

The real Rahal decided to turn the tables on Letterman. He schemed with four of us in the press to get back at the TV star.

"When Letterman comes, I'm going to introduce you as one of the photographers here at Indianapolis," Rahal told me. "Then play like you don't know who he is."

Later that day, Letterman came into the pit area and saw Rahal. Letterman immediately tried to make amends, saying he hoped Rahal wasn't still angry at him for the light bulb skit.

No, said Rahal, he didn't carry a grudge. It was all in fun.

Then Rahal turned and introduced me to Letterman.

"You have a radio show here in Indianapolis?" I innocently asked Letterman.

Letterman said no, not in Indianapolis.

MENARDS

"I have a talk show in New York."

I gave a puzzled look, like I didn't get the connection.

Letterman gave a look of incredulity.

"You don't know who I am?"

I shook my head no.

"I'm on late night TV," Letterman offered, trying to help me make a connection.

"If you're on after 8:30," I deadpanned, "forget it. I'm already in bed."

Letterman's jaw dropped, and he raised his hands in disbelief. When Rahal burst out laughing, Letterman realized he'd been had. I snapped a photo of that moment.

Chippewa Falls connection

Several months later, Letterman began poking fun of a shoe company in Wisconsin.

Letterman told his audience that the company had over 40,000 salesmen, but that the kit they were given contained only one shoe for each style.

"How do they make a living selling one shoe?" Letterman wondered.

The president of the Chippewa Falls-based company, Vic Mason, caught Letterman's show and decided to fire back. He contacted the show's producers, and offered to come to New York to present Letterman with several pairs of shoes.

I found out that Vic and his wife, Bea, would be on Letterman's show. So I printed an 8x10 of Letterman reacting to being punked by Bobby Rahal in Indianapolis.

The show featuring Vic Mason went well. Mason explained how each customer of Mason Shoe Company could in turn become a "salesman" for the firm, and how it sold thousands of pairs of shoes each year via mail order catalogs.

Near the end of his 15 minutes of fame, Mason gave Letterman my photo.

"Oh, don't tell me you're from the same town as him!" Letterman exclaimed.

But he kept the shoes – and the picture.

Page 69: David Letterman, right, surveys the pit area at the Indianapolis Motor Speedway.

Top: Roger Deppe, who handled credentials at the Indy 500 for many years, is shown at the 1988 Indy 500. Deppe would die in a 2005 crash while driving to his vacation home in Minnesota.

Bottom: Driver Bobby Rahal is shown in 1988.

Right: Danica Patrick answers a reporter's question prior to the 2006 Indy 500.

Opposite page: Danica Patrick is shaded from the heat during a pit stop during the practice round of the 2005 Indy 500.

HONDA
AirTran
BBS
BOSCH

Top left: Tim Sullivan is Glenn's most helpful staff member at the Indianpolis Motor Speedway. Tim takes care of the media as part of his job.

Top right: Brent Musburger, who announced the 2007 Indy 500 for ABC, takes a break in the media lunch room.

Left: Scott Dix stands under an umbrella after the 2007 race was called due to rain.

Top: Helio Castroneves's helmet reflect the crowd during the 2007 Indy 500.

Bottom: Felipe Giaffone takes a break during the 2005 Indy 500.

Top: Al Unser, Sr., four time winner of the Indy 500, sits in his race car during the 1992 Indy 500.

Left: Jeff Gordon during a pit stop at the 2002 Brickyard.

Road America – Parking next to a $285,000 Lamborghini in an old pickup truck

This is the story of an old Ford Ranger pickup truck and a new fire engine red Lamborghini.

The year was 2000.

I had dropped off my 1985 Ford Ranger pickup truck at a body shop in Chippewa Falls for a new paint job. Two weeks later, I called the body shop to see if it was ready to go.

I wanted to drive it to the Road America race track outside Elkhart Lake, Wisconsin.

The owner of the body shop said the pickup had been primed a light gray, but the final coat of blue had not yet been applied.

I really needed that pickup truck, because I was going to stop in Appleton on the way back to pick up a piece of furniture.

"No problem," said the body shop owner. "Take the pickup. When you come back, we'll just wash off the dirt and bugs and apply the final coat of paint."

On my way to the race, I drove to Appleton to make sure the piece of furniture was ready for my return trip. Then I headed south, taking the back way to Road America, through classic Wisconsin towns with names like New Holstein.

Pulling in to Road America, I stopped at the old farm house to pick up my media credentials. There, sitting in the lot, was a gorgeous, sexy fire engine red Lamborghini.

For a joke, I pulled alongside the Lamborghini, parking at an angle.

The owner of the Lamborghini popped open the gull wing door on the driver's side and called out, "Why did you pull in on an angle like that?"

Looking nonplussed, I deadpanned, "I don't want you opening your door against my truck. I don't want you to scratch it. It isn't painted yet!"

The Lamborghini owner laughed so hard he almost fell out of his car.

My truck must have been worth a couple thousand dollars, and his Lamborghini – at that time – was worth about $285,000. I never cracked a smile.

The Lamborghini owner wanted a picture taken of the two vehicles and the two owners, standing side by side. A friend came by with a camera and snapped the photo.

Then the Lamborghini owner asked if I wanted to take a ride.

I couldn't get in it. It was down low. He was a skinny little guy, and I wasn't! That car was only so many inches off the ground.

I asked the owner what sort of mileage he got with the Lamborghini.

"If you have to ask, you probably don't want to own one," came the reply.

Top left: Helio Castroneve gives a thumbs up in 2005.

Top right: Lyn St. James is all business as she prepares for the 2000 Indy 500 race.

Left: President of the Indianapolis Motor Speedway, John Cooper (middle), talks with media coordinator, Al Bloemker (left).

Above: Emerson Fittipaldi, winner of the 1989 and 1993 Indy 500, is shown in 1990.

Top left: John Menard is shown at the Austin's White House restaurant in Eau Claire in 1983. A large crowd gathered to view footage of the Spirit of Eau Claire, his first entry into the Indy 500.

Middle left: John Menard is pictured with his son, Chris, at the Michigan International Speedway in 1981.

Bottom left: J.R. Menard and his girlfriend, Laura, at the Brickyard 400 in 2007.

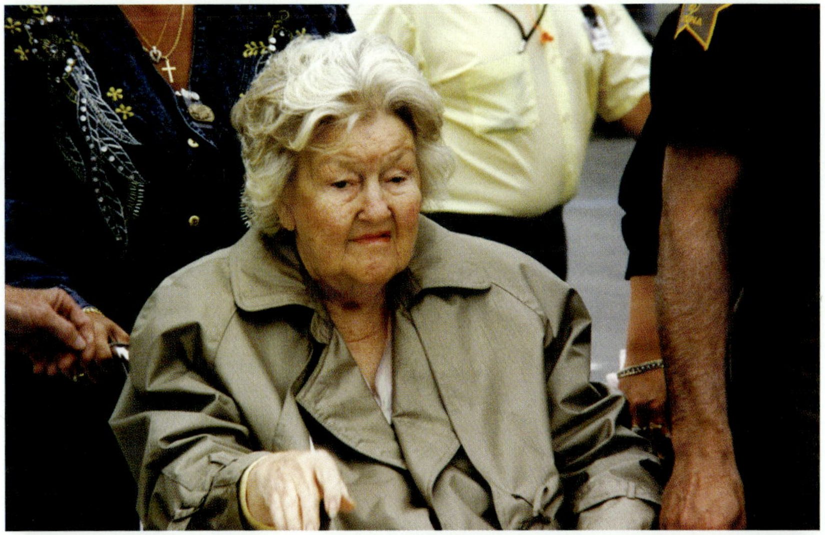

Above: Rick Mears in 1992.

Top right: The farm house at Michigan International Speedway where journalists picked up their credentials.

Middle right: Mary Hulman, owner of the Indianapolis Motor Speedway, is shown in 1996.

Bottom right: Rick Mears, right, is shown in 1989 with his dad, Bill, his brother, Roger, and his mother, Skip.

Top left: Jeff Gordon climbs into his car at the Brickyard 400 in 2005.

Top right: Tony George, president of the Indianapolis Motor Speedway, and Bill France, chairman of NASCAR, visit in 2003.

Right: Al Unser, Jr. and Bobby Rahal are in the pits together at the Michigan International Speedway.

Top left: Arie Luyendyk, Jr. in 1991.

Top right: Roger Penske in 1979.

Left: Richard Petty in 1989.

Left: John Menard and his daughter, Molly Menard, pose at the Brickyard 400 in 2007.

John Menard, a local kid who made good in business and racing

John Menard is a self-made man. He did it by working hard.

His business – Menards – is known throughout the country as the place for do-it-yourselfers who want to "save big money." What a great slogan.

I met John shortly after he opened his first hardware store in 1972 in his hometown of Eau Claire, Wisconsin, which is just downriver from Chippewa Falls. I took some pictures for John to be used in his newspaper advertisements.

But I really got to know John when he put together a race team to compete in the Indy 500. The car, called the "Spirit of Eau Claire," was driven by Herm Johnson. Since I was at Indianapolis covering the race for the Chippewa Herald-Telegram, I took photos and footage of the Spirit of Eau Claire.

Later, during the cold winter months, I would show the film at the White House restaurant in Eau Claire. The film generated a lot of interest and excitement in racing and in the Spirit of Eau Claire. The White House was full the nights we showed it. Several other business owners, including auto dealer Lee Markquart, signed on to co-sponsor the racing team with John.

Since I was covering the races for my hometown newspaper, I was bound and determined to cover anything John did in the field of auto racing. Over the years, I was fortunate to shoot hundreds of photos of the Menards car, race team and of John and his family.

At the racetrack, John is inconspicuously around, watching and anticipating what will be needed next. He helps here and there, yet he doesn't want, or look for, recognition. He's a thinking man who reacts to what's going on.

I never have to worry about a goof-up with my press credentials, although it's happened on occasion. Just a simple call to John solves the problem right away. He's been great to me.

You may not realize it, but John hires many people in the Midwest to work for his company. At one point, other communities outside of Wisconsin tried to lure John's corporate headquarters away from Eau Claire. Instead of moving his headquarters to more central location in the U.S., where it would have been better for the whole operation, he stayed here. He loves his hometown.

His concern for his family is a wonderful example of a good dad. I admire all his kids and know they'll carry on with his example.

Of course, his best attribute is his love of racing. Since that initial sponsorship of the "Spirit of Eau Claire," he continues to keep an interest in the sport. Nowadays, he sponsors his son, Paul, in NASCAR, and still maintains ownership in Indy cars.

Keep up the good work, John.

Above: Menard's Racing Team sponsored three cars in the 1992 Indy 500. Drivers were, left to right, Gary Bettenhausen, Al Unser, Sr., and Tom Sneva.

Right: A fish eye shot of the 2000 Menard's car driven by Robby Gordon.

MENARDS
JM
Johns Manville
MENARDS
JM
Johns Manville
MENARDS

Opposite page: Pit stop, 2004, Milwauke Mile.

Top: John Menard, left, visits with Robbie Buhl at the 1998 Indy 500.

Middle: Paul Menard takes a break during the 2006 Brickyard just prior to his qualifying run.

Bottom: The Team Menard car at Disney World in 2000.

Top left: John Menard, center, in the pit area of the Brickyard in 2007.

Top right: Paul Menard comes in from a practice run at the Brickyard in 2007.

Left: The Menard's car at the Indy 500 in 1997.

Right: Townsend Bell drove for Team Menards at the Milwaukee Mile in 2004.

Final thoughts

Just imagine the changes I've seen since 1946 at Indianapolis. Those early cars were so different from one another. If you built a race car, it could be entered in the competition.

Even before that (the 1920s), a mechanic or two rode with the driver to keep the car running at its best. In the 1930s, open wheel (sprint) cars were the norm, but the 1940s brought the roadster.

Captain Eddie Rickenbacker owned the track during the war years, 1942-45. No races were held during those years, and the track was in poor condition. In 1945, Tony Hulman bought the Indy race track and strove to bring it back into good shape. He was a very gracious and conscientious man, who checked with me on a regular basis to see if everything was OK.

When Tony Hulman's grandson, Tony George, took over the Indianapolis Motor Speedway in 1989, he continued to build both the track and goodwill. There is a world of difference between 1945 and the present in the speedway. Sometimes, I must admit, I am nostalgic for the earlier, friendlier and simpler years.

In my early years, we reporters and photographers were based under the grandstand on the main straight-away (maybe 20 or so worked at the racetrack then). Later, we moved across to the main building – a huge improvement. Suddenly, our small group grew to about 100 members of the news media.

Finally, we were moved to the new Media Center at Indy. The steel-and-glass building is four stories high, with all the modern mish-mash of phones, computers, monitors and rows upon rows of desks – accommodating perhaps 400 members of the press.

What a great time it was when NASCAR came to Indy in 1994. John Cooper, the president of the speedway, worked very hard to make that happen. That was an excellent move on the speedway's part, sponsoring the Brickyard 400. Because some of the early races took place on brick roads, a small patch of bricks was left at the finish line as a remembrance of those first races.

Also, I'll fondly remember the Formula One cars that raced at the speedway for five years – a demanding bunch!

Ethanol was used to fuel the cars for the last few years. It's great that they're not using regular gas. I hope an alternative fuel is perfected soon for all of us.

I am one lucky fellow. It's been an enriching experience, growing and changing with racing these last 60 years. I've enjoyed the support given me by my three sons and wife over all these years. It was especially great when my youngest, Wade, was able to accompany me for 15 years to photograph races at Indy. What a life! I thank God.

Right: Here is a picture of my wife, Arla, at the inaugural races at Disney World in Orlanda in 1996.

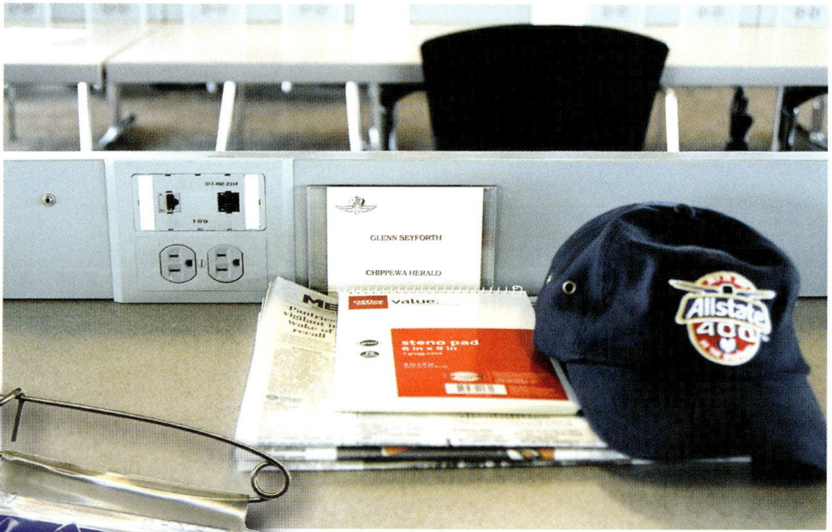

Above: A.J. Foyt at Road America in Elkhart Lake, Wiscondin, one hour before his crash in 1988.

Top right: My "three amigos," Tom, Roscoe and Mike are always there for me during the Indy 500.

Right: My seat in the media room at Indianapolis, and my first credentials issued by former Herald-Telegram owner John Lavine.